Gallery Books
Editor Peter Fallon

THE DEAD, 1904

Paul Muldoon
Jean Hanff Korelitz

THE DEAD, 1904

An adaptation of
The Dead by James Joyce

Gallery Books

The Dead, 1904
was first published
simultaneously in paperback
and in a clothbound edition
on 17 November 2018.

The Gallery Press
Loughcrew
Oldcastle
County Meath
Ireland

www.gallerypress.com

ISBN 978 1 91133 757 7 *paperback*
978 1 91133 758 4 *clothbound*

A CIP catalogue record for this book
is available from the British Library.

The Dead, 1904 receives financial assistance
from the Arts Council.

for Bono and Ali

Characters

GABRIEL CONROY, a teacher and book reviewer
MARY JANE MORKAN, a music teacher
KATE MORKAN ⎱ Gabriel and Mary Jane's aunts, elderly sisters,
JULIA MORKAN ⎰ music teachers, who throw a party every year
          on January 6th, the Feast of the Epiphany
LILY, the caretaker's daughter, maid to the Misses Morkan
MOLLY IVORS, classmate of Gabriel from university, feminist
   and patriot
GRETTA CONROY, Gabriel's wife
MR BROWNE, only Protestant guest at the party
FREDDY MALINS, an alcoholic and friend of Gabriel
MRS MALINS, Freddy's mother
BARTELL D'ARCY, famous tenor
MISS DALY, student of Mary Jane (musician: piano, violin/fiddle,
   preferably both)

Setting

Entryway/Lobby (Suggested: Ground Floor)
Parlour (Suggested: 1st Floor)
Dining Room (Suggested: 1st Floor)
Bedroom (Suggested: 2nd Floor)

Staging may vary based on the building in which the play is being presented.

For notes on alternate setting see page 54

The Dead, 1904 was first produced by Dot Dot Productions LLC (Nina Korelitz Matza and Jean Hanff Korelitz), Laurie Eustis and Kathleen Begala in association with The American Irish Historical Society for The Irish Repertory Theatre. Presented at The American Irish Historical Society in New York City from November 2016 to January 2017, with the following cast:

GABRIEL CONROY	Boyd Gaines
MARY JANE MORKAN	Barrie Kreinik
KATE MORKAN	Patricia Kilgarriff
JULIA MORKAN	Patti Perkins
LILY	Clare O'Malley
MOLLY IVORS	Aedin Moloney
GRETTA CONROY	Kate Burton
MR BROWNE	Peter Cormican
FREDDY MALINS	James Russell
MRS MALINS	Terry Donnelly
BARTELL D'ARCY	Karl Scully
MISS DALY	Heather Martin Bixler

Director	Ciaran O'Reilly
Costumes	Leon Dobkowsky
Lighting Design	Michael Gottlieb
Choreography	Barry McNabb
Sound Design	M. Florian Staab
Properties and	
Interior Design	Deirdre Brennan
Hair and Wigs	Robert-Charles Vallance
Dialect Consultant	Stephen Gabis
Music Consultant	Mark Hartman

A note on The Dead, 1904 *as immersive theatre*

At *The Dead, 1904*, audience members do not sit and observe as they would in a conventional theatre. Instead, they participate in the performance as silent party guests at the Morkan sisters' Feast of the Epiphany celebration, held annually on January 6th and taking place on this night, January 6th, 1904. The action proceeds in real time, without intermission, and includes music, dance, food and drink. Audience members move between rooms as the evening unfolds, drinking and eating alongside the characters, and following in-character guidance from the cast members. We have found that, as immersive theatre is more frequently created and attended, audience members have become sophisticated observers and participants, and are able to enjoy the evening with little or no overt manipulation.

A note on performance space

The Dead, 1904 was initially written for and produced at The American Irish Historical Society, a c.1900 Beaux Arts mansion located in New York City and, as a result, some stage directions pertaining to the arrangement of rooms are based on the physical layout of that particular space. In subsequent productions of the play adjustments may be made as to layout and movement, though the effort should always be to suggest a period-appropriate home, of multiple storeys, that will include the following primary performance areas:

parlour: opening scene, post-dinner scene
dining room: dinner scene
bedroom: final scene, ideally up a flight of stairs from the
    parlour and dining spaces

A note on audience accommodations and guidelines

While most audience members stand during the parlour and bedroom scenes we place chairs in these rooms for people who need or wish to sit, and we accommodate those who cannot climb stairs with an elevator between floors. During dinner everyone is seated to share the meal.

For notes on food and seating arrangements see page 58

For notes on music see page 60

PART ONE

Prologue

(Staging Note: Because The American Irish Historical Society has a large lobby with a cloakroom we chose to have audience members gather there. The play begins as LILY *the housemaid descends the stairs to greet them and invite them to join the 'party' upstairs in the first floor parlour area.)*

As audience members enter the parlour they are offered drinks by the waitstaff (whiskey, sherry, stout, punch) and greeted by cast members. During the 15-minute 'Prologue' that follows audience members are free to wander around the parlour floor, speaking to one another and to those cast members present (all apart from Gabriel, Gretta and Freddy). They are unnamed guests at the Misses Morkan's holiday party, and spoken to familiarly by cast members. They may draw close to the piano as music is played and sung by MISS DALY, MARY JANE, MR BROWNE, *and even* LILY. *Some audience members may even accept an invitation to dance from a cast member (*MR BROWNE, MRS MALLINS, BARTELL D'ARCY, MOLLY IVORS*).*

The action is only lightly scripted at this point, but includes the following:

AUNT KATE *fusses about Gabriel's arrival, asking audience members and cast members alike:* Is he here yet? Is Gabriel here? Have you seen my nephew?

AUNT KATE *and* AUNT JULIA *carry plates of food through the audience to the dining room where they can be seen fussing over the tables.*

MR BROWNE *asks women from the audience to dance.*

MOLLY IVORS *asks men from the audience to dance.*

MRS MALLINS *asks men from the audience to dance.*

LILY, AUNT KATE, AUNT JULIA *or* MARY JANE *may guide an audience member to a chair.*

Cast members may ask: Is this your first time at the Misses Morkan's party? Is Gabriel going to make a speech at dinner tonight? Isn't the snow dreadful?

At the piano, music is played in this order:
MISS DALY *and* MARY JANE *play a sample of Moore's* Melodies *on the piano.* MARY JANE *accompanies* AUNT JULIA *as she practises the song she'll later perform: 'Arrayed for the Bridal'.*

MR BROWNE, MARY JANE *and* MISS DALY *sing a popular tune.* MR BROWNE *calls* LILY *over to the piano to join them and* LILY *gets through a single solo verse before* AUNT KATE *comes storming over to the piano, hissing* 'Lily! Get back downstairs!'

Cast members mark the end of MARY JANE*'s final song with an extra enthusiastic round of applause which focuses audience attention, at which point* LILY *emerges at the head of the stairs with the play's true opening line.*

LILY   I am run off my feet. Literally run off my feet!
KATE   Is he here yet, Lily? Is Gabriel here?
LILY   (*Exasperated*) No, Miss Kate, not yet.

> *Immediately, she hears something from the bottom of the stairs and calls down to the newcomers:*

> Oh, Mr Con-uh-roy. Miss Kate and Miss Julia thought you were never coming. (*As they enter*) Goodnight, Mrs Con-uh-roy.

> GRETTA *ascends to parlour.* GABRIEL *lags a few steps behind.*

GABRIEL   I'll engage they did. But they forget that my wife here takes three mortal hours to dress herself.
LILY   Miss Kate! Miss Julia! Here's Mrs Con-uh-roy!

> JULIA *and* KATE *come briskly to the head of the stairs. Both kiss* GRETTA.

KATE   You must be perished alive!
JULIA   Is Gabriel with you?
GABRIEL   Here I am, as right as the mail, Aunt Julia! Go on up, I'll follow.

All three women ascend the stairs to the next floor,
disappearing from sight, laughing together. GABRIEL
sits at the edge of the parlour to remove his galoshes,
and LILY *kneels at his feet to assist.*

LILY Is it snowing again, Mr Con-uh-roy?

GABRIEL Yes, Lily, and I think we're in for a night of it.
Con-uh-roy. You make me sound like some ancient
Irish king.

LILY Miss Kate always says your mother was the
brains-carrier of the family.

GABRIEL Conroy. Two syllables are quite enough. Tell me,
Lily, do you still go to school?

LILY Oh no, sir. I'm done schooling this year and more.

GABRIEL Oh then, I suppose we'll be going to your wedding
one of these fine days with your young man, eh?

LILY (*Bitterly*) The men that is now is only all palaver
and what they can get out of you.

GABRIEL *is embarrassed, aware that he has said*
something wrong, but unclear as to what. He kicks at
his galoshes to get them off, adjusts his clothing. He
fumbles for a coin in his pocket.

GABRIEL Oh Lily, it's Christmastime, isn't it? Just . . . here's
a little . . .

LILY Oh no, sir! I wouldn't take it.

GABRIEL, *escaping quickly, waves at* LILY.

GABRIEL Christmastime! Christmastime!

LILY Well, thank you, sir.

MRS MALINS *and* MR D'ARCY *make their way through*
the crowd towards the centre of the room.

MRS MALINS Oh, Mr D'Arcy, it's always such a great affair. Never
once has it fallen flat.

MR D'ARCY Yes, I'm told it has gone off in splendid style as long as anyone can remember.

MRS MALINS Ever since Kate and Julia left the house in Stoney Batter and took Mary Jane to live with them here on Usher's Island.

MR D'ARCY Mary Jane's their niece?

MRS MALINS Mary Jane's their niece . . . That was a good thirty years ago if it was a day.

MARY JANE (*Overhearing her name mentioned*) Good evening, Mrs Malins. And good evening, Mr D'Arcy. We're so pleased you could attend this evening. Do you think you might favour us with a rendition? I know my pupils would adore that.

MR D'ARCY I'm as hoarse as a crow, Miss Mary Jane. Hoarse as a crow.

MRS MALINS I suppose, Mary Jane, most of your pupils belong to better-class families.

MARY JANE They do indeed. Most of them are on the Kingstown and Dalkey line.

MRS MALINS It's so wonderful to think that Julia is still the leading soprano in Adam and Eve's.

MR D'ARCY And Miss Kate gives music lessons to beginners on that old piano.

MARY JANE We both give music lessons, Mr D'Arcy. That's our bread and butter.

MRS MALINS (*Unthinkingly*) Gabriel has always been their favourite nephew.

MARY JANE I think you could say that, Mrs Malins. I think you could say that.

MRS MALINS You know I always liked their dead elder sister, Ellen, who married T J Conroy.

MARY JANE (*Clarifying*) T J Conroy of the Port and Docks.

MR D'ARCY So he enjoyed a certain position in society.

MARY JANE He certainly did!

KATE, JULIA *and* GRETTA *descend the stairs and return to the party.*

KATE Gretta tells me you're not going to take a cab back to Monkstown tonight, Gabriel.

GABRIEL   No, we had quite enough of that last year, hadn't we? Don't you remember, Aunt Kate, what a cold poor Gretta got out of it? Cab windows rattling all the way, and the east wind blowing in after we passed Merrion. Very jolly it was. Gretta caught a dreadful cold.

KATE   Quite right, Gabriel, quite right. You can't be too careful.

GABRIEL   As for Gretta there, she'd walk home in the snow if she were let.

GRETTA   Don't mind him, Aunt Kate. He's really an awful bother with the children, what with green shades for Tom's eyes at night and making him do the dumb-bells and forcing Eva to eat the stirabout. The poor child! And she simply hates the sight of it! Oh, but you'll never guess what he makes me wear now! (*Pause*) Galoshes! That's the latest. Whenever it's wet underfoot I must put on my galoshes. Tonight even, he wanted me to put them on, but I wouldn't. The next thing he'll buy me will be a diving suit.

JULIA   And what are galoshes, Gabriel?

KATE   Galoshes, Julia! Goodness me, don't you know what galoshes are? You wear them over your . . . over your boots, Gretta, isn't it?

GRETTA   Yes. Guttapercha things. We both have a pair now. Gabriel says everyone wears them on the Continent.

JULIA   (*Nodding*) Oh, on the Continent!

      JULIA *drifts away and goes to the top of the staircase, leaning out over the banister to look downstairs.*

GABRIEL   It's nothing very wonderful, but Gretta thinks it very funny because she says the word reminds her of Christy Minstrels.

KATE   Now, now. Let's not make a terrible *faux pas*.

GABRIEL   Let's not, by gosh!

GRETTA   Gabriel, you sound like someone out of a penny

dreadful. (*Changing the subject*) It's so good of you to let us stay the night. I know it's a terrible fuss with the house full.

KATE The house won't be quite so full as it's been. Mr Browne is leaving tonight. (*Sotto voce*) He's been laid on here like the gas throughout the Christmas season! Lily has made up your bed in the front room. It isn't fancy.

GABRIEL I had been hoping to stay at the Gresham Hotel. A night away from the children. You know?

GRETTA This is no less a hostelry.

KATE And the children, Gretta. You're not anxious about them?

GRETTA Oh, not for one night. Besides, Bessie will look after them.

KATE What a comfort, to have a girl like that, one you can depend on! There's that Lily. I'm not sure what has come over her lately. She's not the girl she was at all. (*Looking over at her sister*) Now I ask you, where is Julia going? Julia! Julia! Where are you going?

JULIA Here's Freddy. Slip down, Gabriel, like a good fellow, and see if he's all right, and don't let him up if he's screwed. I'm sure he's screwed. I'm sure he is.

GABRIEL *crosses to the top of the stairs and listens. From downstairs all hear* FREDDY MALINS *laughing.*

KATE (*To* GRETTA) It's such a relief that Gabriel is here. I always feel easier in my mind when he's here. Julia, Miss Daly will take some refreshment. Thanks for your beautiful waltz, Miss Daly. It made lovely time. Didn't it, Mr Browne?

MR BROWNE *is staring at* MISS IVORS' *bodice.*

MR BROWNE It did indeed, indeed it did. Oh, Miss Ivors, I wonder if I may broach the subject of your . . . brooch.

MISS IVORS It's an Irish device, Mr Browne.

MR BROWNE An Irish device. And the motto? Also Irish?
MISS IVORS *Tír agus Teanga.* 'Land and Language.' The two are bound up.
MR BROWNE Oh, inextricably. I'm the man for the ladies. You know, Miss Morkan, there's a reason they're so fond of me.
JULIA (*To* MISS DALY) I've a nice partner for you, Mr Bartell D'Arcy, the tenor. I'll get him to sing later on. All Dublin is raving about him.
KATE Lovely voice, lovely voice! (*To* JULIA) What is the matter, Julia? Who is it?
JULIA It's only Freddy, Kate. And Gabriel with him.

GABRIEL *descends the stairs and pilots* FREDDY MALINS *back up and across the parlour.* FREDDY *is laughing heartily and looks sleepy, halfway through a story and rubbing his fist into his eye.*

Good evening, Freddy.

FREDDY *greets* JULIA *and* KATE *in an offhand manner and goes to a male guest and repeats the story he has evidently just told* GABRIEL.

FREDDY Usher was what she was saying, it must have been. Usher in. Like at a wedding or a funeral. Usher in to Usher's Island.
KATE (*To* GABRIEL) He's not so bad, is he?
GABRIEL Oh, no. Hardly noticeable.
MR BROWNE (*To* FREDDY) Now then, Teddy, I'm going to fill you out a good glass of lemonade, just to buck you up.

FREDDY, *still enthusiastically telling his story, extends his hand automatically and takes the glass without pausing. Reaching the story's climax he explodes in high-pitched laughter, rubbing his eye once again.*

But I thought she said, 'Push her in.' Do you see what I mean? I thought she said, 'Push her in'!

21

KATE Now isn't he a terrible fellow! And his poor mother made him take the pledge on New Year's Eve. So much for total abstinence! Well . . . I think . . . a little music? Miss Daly? Would you favour us with your Academy piece?

MISS DALY *plays the violin (alternately, the piano) to a hushed room. It is a showy, complex piece of music, full of frills and dramatic displays.* KATE *stands by to turn the pages. Applause as the piece ends.*

Quadrilles! Quadrilles! May I get you a partner, Miss Daly? We're so short of ladies tonight. You're really awfully good, after playing for the last however many dances.

MISS DALY I don't mind in the least, Miss Morkan.

MISS DALY *finds dance music. The dance begins.*
GABRIEL *is partnered with* MISS IVORS.

MISS IVORS (*As they are preparing to dance*) I have a crow to pluck with you.
GABRIEL With me? What is it?
MISS IVORS (*Nodding*) Who is GC?

GABRIEL *frowns but says nothing.*

Oh, Innocent Amy! I have found out that you write for the *Daily Express*. Now, aren't you ashamed of yourself?
GABRIEL Why should I be ashamed of myself?
MISS IVORS Well, I'm ashamed of you. To say you'd write for an anti-Irish rag like that. I didn't think you were a West Briton.
GABRIEL It's true I write a literary column every Wednesday in the *Daily Express*. That doesn't make me a West Briton. There's nothing political in writing reviews of books. Browning. *When We Dead Awaken. The Poetical Works of Bret Harte.*

GABRIEL *and* MISS IVORS *dance uncomfortably.*

MISS IVORS Of course I was only joking. A friend of mine
showed me your review of Browning. (*Quoting
from the review*) 'One feels that one is listening to a
thought-tormented music.' I like that. A little pre-
tentious but I do like it immensely. That was how
I found out your secret . . . Come, we cross now.

MR BROWNE *and* FREDDY MALINS *hold themselves
slightly apart from the festivities.*

MR BROWNE I tell you, Teddy.
FREDDY Freddy.
MR BROWNE It's the doctor's orders.
FREDDY Oh, well now, Mr Browne, I'm sure the doctor never
ordered anything of the kind.
MR BROWNE Well, I'm like the famous Mrs Cassidy who is
reported to have said, 'Now, Mary Grimes, if I don't
take it, make me take it, for I feel I want it.'
FREDDY Would you take a gander at Julia and Kate?
MR BROWNE Sometimes I wonder if they're not just two ignorant
old women.
FREDDY That's a terrible thing to say. You're a guest in
their house. You've been here for a week.
MR BROWNE But all of this, it's only for show.
FREDDY Isn't the Feast of the Epiphany all about show?
The showing forth of the Infant Jesus? You're a gas
man, Mr Browne.
MR BROWNE I hear tell I've been laid on like the gas in this
house right through the Christmas period. Now
they're putting me out on the street. So much for
Irish hospitality!
FREDDY Because now they don't even own this house.
They rent the upper part from Mr Fulham, the
corn factor on the ground floor.
MR BROWNE What's a corn factor when he's at home?
FREDDY The fact is Mary Jane is now the main prop of the
household for she has the organ in Haddington

23

Road. Mary Jane has been through the Academy and gives a pupils' concert every year in the Ancient Concert Rooms. But their life is modest. Most modest.

MR BROWNE Their life may be modest but they believe in eating well; the best of everything: diamond-bone sirloins, three-shilling tea and the best bottled stout. It's true I've been the beneficiary of all that.

FREDDY Stout? Did you say stout? Some of us are ready for bottle or draught.

MISS IVORS Oh, Mr Conroy, will you come for an excursion to the Aran Isles this summer? We're going to stay there a whole month. It will be splendid out in the Atlantic. You ought to come. Mr Clancy is coming, and Mr Kilkelly and Kathleen Kearney. It would be splendid for Gretta too if she'd come. She's from Connacht, isn't she?

GABRIEL Her people are.

MISS IVORS But you will come, won't you?

GABRIEL The fact is, I have just arranged to go . . .

MISS IVORS Go where?

GABRIEL Well, you know, every year I go for a cycling tour with some fellows . . .

MISS IVORS But where?

GABRIEL Well, we usually go to France or Belgium or perhaps Germany.

MISS IVORS And why do you go to France or Belgium, instead of visiting your own land?

GABRIEL Well, it's partly to keep in touch with the languages and partly for a change.

MISS IVORS And haven't you your own language to keep in touch with? Irish?

GABRIEL Well, if it comes to that, you know, Irish is not my language.

As the conversation becomes more heated other dancers begin to watch and listen.

MISS IVORS So you won't have been to *Muirgheis*?

GABRIEL The Irish opera. *Muirgheis*. What does that mean?
MISS IVORS *Muir* is the word for sea. It's like *mare* in Latin.
Don't you remember any of this from University?
And *geis* or *geas* is a word that means something
like a taboo or an imprecation.
GABRIEL Gas?
MISS IVORS (*Correcting his pronunciation*) *Geis. Faoi gheasa* means
something like 'under a spell'. Haven't you your
own land to visit, that you know nothing of, your
own people and your own country?
GABRIEL Oh, to tell you the truth, I'm sick of my own country,
sick of it!
MISS IVORS Why?

The dance formation interrupts them; GABRIEL, *irked,
does not answer.*

Why? Of course, you've no answer.

GABRIEL, *ignoring her, dances with great energy, avoid-
ing her eyes. The formation is about to start again.*

(*Dismissively*) West Briton!

The dance ends. GABRIEL *escapes to a corner of the
room where* MRS MALINS *is now sitting.*

GABRIEL So, Mrs Malins, you know Freddy finally got here?
MRS MALINS I heard that. Is he bad?
GABRIEL Oh, no. Hardly noticeable.

GRETTA *and* MISS IVORS *find themselves face to face.*

MISS IVORS (*Slightly flustered*) Dia dhuit.
GRETTA Dia agus Muire dhuit.
MISS IVORS Gretta, I'm terribly afraid Gabriel and I had words.
GRETTA Yes. We noticed. Did you enjoy that?
MISS IVORS Enjoy?
GRETTA Stirring the pot.

MISS IVORS I was praising his work in the *Daily Express* — an imperial rag beneath his powers. Last week he gave his entire column to that strange novel by Bret Harte about the California gold rush.

GRETTA My husband has universal tastes. 'Go west, young man.'

MISS IVORS I just wish if he was going to write about starvation and cannibalism in 1847, that he would look no further than his own country. *Maireann an chraobh ar an bhfál ach ní mhaireann an lámh do chuir.* It means . . .

GRETTA I know what it means, Molly. 'The branch lives on the hedge though the hand that planted it be dead.' Listen, my mother was about ten years of age in 1847. She talked once, and once only, about the hard times in Gort.

MISS IVORS Gort? Wasn't that Lord Gregory's home turf?

GRETTA It certainly was. Lord Gregory wouldn't allow anyone who owned more than a quarter acre of land to get any kind of relief . . . The story my mother told, I don't remember the ins and outs of it, but I do remember that a starving woman had eaten part of the leg and foot of one of her own children.

MISS IVORS Lord Gregory still has a very bad name in the West, Gretta. I only wish Gabriel would write about that . . .

GRETTA Yes, Molly, but there's a time and a place . . .

GABRIEL *is intent on* MRS MALINS.

GABRIEL Did you have a good crossing, Mrs Malins?

MRS MALINS A beautiful crossing. The captain was most attentive to me. You know I live in Glasgow with my daughter. She keeps a beautiful house in Glasgow. Beautiful. I come back to Dublin on a visit just once a year.

GABRIEL Once a year may be once too often.

MRS MALINS Every year my son-in-law brings us to the Highlands. The beauty of the Highlands is that you can

26

go for half a day without coming upon a soul.

MR BROWNE (*Overhearing this*) There's a reason for that, Mrs Malins. There's a very good reason for that. My ancestors are from the Highlands. They were cleared off the land to make way for sheep. Dispossessed. Dispossession is something that seems to run in my blood. My family moved to Ayrshire. I should say we were forced to move to Ayrshire. We're almost certainly related to Robert Burns. On his mother's side, of course.

GABRIEL Of course. That's the sort of detail that's so often lost, Mr Browne. The smallest actions may have the greatest consequences.

MR BROWNE 'Take us the foxes', Gabriel, 'the little foxes that spoil the vines.'

MRS MALINS Is he bad, Gabriel?

GABRIEL Hardly noticeable, Mrs Malins.

GRETTA (*Approaching* GABRIEL) Gabriel, Aunt Kate wants to know won't you carve the goose as usual? Miss Daly will carve the ham and I'll do the pudding.

GABRIEL All right. Were you dancing?

GRETTA Of course I was! Didn't you see me? What words had you with Molly Ivors?

GABRIEL No words. Why? Did she say so?

GRETTA Something like that. I'm trying to get that Mr D'Arcy to sing. He's full of conceit, I think.

GABRIEL There were no words, only she wanted me to go on a trip to the West of Ireland and I said I wouldn't.

GRETTA (*Excitedly*) Oh, do let's go, Gabriel! I'd love to see Galway again!

GABRIEL You can go if you like.

GRETTA (*To* MRS MALINS) There's a nice husband for you, Mrs Malins.

MRS MALINS My daughter in Scotland has the loveliest husband! A lovelier fellow you wouldn't meet in a day's march. Every year he brings us to the Highlands and we go fishing. He's a splendid fisher. Once he caught a fish — a beautiful big, big fish — and the man in the hotel boiled it for our dinner.

GRETTA *leaves, heading back towards the dining room. She crosses paths with* FREDDY MALINS *who approaches his mother.* GABRIEL *gets up and gives his chair to* FREDDY. *He takes out the paper from his waistcoat and again goes over his speech.*

GRETTA Ladies and Gentlemen, Aunt Kate!

KATE And now . . . a wonderful surprise! I have per-suaded my sister to sing! Yes, and it wasn't an easy thing to coax her, I assure you. Where is Mary Jane? Our niece Mary Jane will accompany. Here, for your delectation!

MARY JANE *begins to play, accompanying* JULIA *on the piano.*

JULIA 'Arrayed for the bridal, in beauty behold her,
A white wreath entwineth a forehead more fair;
I envy the zephyrs that softly enfold her, enfold her,
And play with the locks of her beautiful hair.
May life to her prove full of sunshine and love, of love yes! yes! yes!
Who would not love her?
Sweet star of the morning! shining so bright,
Earth's circle adorning, fair creature of light! Fair creature of light.'

When she finishes all applaud loudly. JULIA *bends to gather up her old leather-bound songbook.* FREDDY *continues to applaud after others have stopped. He stands up suddenly.*

FREDDY I was just telling my mother, I never heard you sing so well, never! No, I never heard your voice so good as it is tonight. Now! Would you believe that now? That's the truth. Upon my word and honour, that's the truth. I never heard your voice sound so fresh and so . . . so clear and fresh, never.

JULIA *smiles and tries to extract her hand.*

MR BROWNE Miss Julia Morkan, my latest discovery!

FREDDY Well, Browne, if you're serious you might make a worse discovery. All I can say is I never heard her sing half so well as long as I'm coming here. And that's the honest truth.

MR BROWNE Neither did I. I think her voice has greatly improved.

JULIA (*Shrugging*) Thirty years ago I hadn't a bad voice, as voices go.

KATE I often told Julia that she was simply thrown away in that choir. But she never would be said by me. No, she wouldn't be said or led by anyone, slaving there in that choir night and day, night and day. Six o'clock on Christmas morning! And all for what?

MARY JANE (*From the piano*) Well, isn't it for the honour of God, Aunt Kate?

KATE I know all about the honour of God, Mary Jane, but I think it's not at all honourable for the Pope to turn the women out of the choirs that have slaved there all their lives and put little whippersnappers of boys over their heads. I suppose it is for the good of the Church if the Pope does it. But it's not just, Mary Jane, and it's not right.

MARY JANE Now, Aunt Kate, you're giving scandal to Mr Browne who is of the other persuasion.

KATE (*To* MR BROWNE) Oh, I don't question the Pope's being right. I'm only a stupid old woman and I wouldn't presume to do such a thing. But there's also such a thing as common everyday politeness and gratitude. And if I were in Julia's place I'd tell that Father Healy straight up to his face . . . Well, we really are all hungry and when we are hungry we are all very quarrelsome.

MR BROWNE And when we are thirsty we are also quarrelsome.

MARY JANE So that we had better go to supper, and finish the discussion afterwards. Mr D'Arcy, would you be so good as to take Miss Daly in.

MR D'ARCY Miss Daly, may I accompany you to your seat?

MISS DALY Mr D'Arcy, I thank you.

MARY JANE (*Joining* GABRIEL) I wonder what Constantine makes of it all?

GABRIEL Constantine?

MARY JANE Your brother!

GABRIEL My brother.

MARY JANE You seem to have forgotten that he's senior curate in Balbriggan.

GABRIEL ignores her. He is gazing at various artefacts on the wall.

GABRIEL The princes. The princes in the tower . . . That needlepoint by my mother. And that photograph of my mother. She holds an open book on her knees and is pointing out something in it to Constantine. He's dressed in a man-o'-war suit. He's lying at her feet. For one year she had worked on a birthday present for me of a waistcoat of purple tabinet, with little foxes' heads upon it, lined with brown satin and having round mulberry buttons. It was she who chose our names, Constantine and Gabriel, for she was very sensible of the dignity of family life. The princes in the tower. She once spoke of Gretta as being country cute and that wasn't true of Gretta at all. It was Gretta who nursed her during her last long illness in our house in Monkstown.

MARY JANE (*Breaking* GABRIEL's *reverie*) We had better go to supper.

GRETTA and MARY JANE are trying to persuade MISS IVORS to stay for dinner. MISS IVORS has put on her hat and is buttoning her cloak.

MISS IVORS But I don't feel the least bit hungry. And I've already overstayed my time.

GRETTA But only for ten minutes, Molly. That won't delay you.

MARY JANE To take a pick itself, after all your dancing.

MISS IVORS I really couldn't.

MARY JANE I am afraid you didn't enjoy yourself at all.

MISS IVORS Ever so much, I assure you. But you really must let me run off now.

GRETTA But how can you get home?

MISS IVORS Oh, it's only two steps up the quay.

GABRIEL If you will allow me, Miss Ivors, I'll see you home if you are really obliged to go.

MISS IVORS (*Breaking away*) I won't hear of it. For goodness' sake go in to your suppers and don't mind me. I'm quite well able to take care of myself.

GRETTA Well, you're the comical girl, Molly.

MISS IVORS *Beannacht libh.*

She descends the staircase with a flourish.

LILY Ladies and Gentlemen, the Misses Morkan are wanting to serve the dinner! Please would everybody join us in the dining room . . .

PART TWO

Dinner. Dining Room.

KATE Where is Gabriel? Where on earth is Gabriel? There's everyone waiting in there, stage to let, and nobody to carve the goose.

GABRIEL Here I am, Aunt Kate! Ready to carve a flock of geese, if necessary.

> GABRIEL *takes his place at the main table and begins to carve.*

Mrs Malins, what shall I send you? A wing or a slice of the breast?

MRS MALINS Just a small slice of the breast.

GABRIEL Aunt Julia, what for you?

JULIA Oh, anything at all.

> KATE, MARY JANE *and* LILY *continue to fuss around, offering more food.*

FREDDY Would you listen to them? 'Anything at all.'

MR BROWNE It's all or nothing. The goose, the ham, the spiced beef. The raisins and almonds. The Smyrna figs. The custard topped with grated nutmeg. It's either a feast or a famine. But it's what isn't here I'm thinking of.

MARY JANE Well, I'll say what isn't here — the applesauce! It's my belief you can't have goose without applesauce, but Julia told me no. She told me roast goose without applesauce has always been good enough for her!

JULIA And I hope I might never eat worse!

FREDDY Never! It's a capital meal! Every year. And the

company! Capital. Miss Mary Jane! Give us your party piece!

MARY JANE Now, don't be putting me on the spot.

GABRIEL Come on, Mary Jane. Give us a recitation.

MARY JANE Not now, Freddy! Maybe later!

GABRIEL Now, if anyone wants a little more of what the vulgar people call 'spuds' let him or her speak.

All encourage him to sit and begin his own meal.
LILY continues to serve both actors and guests.

Very well, kindly forget my existence, Ladies and Gentlemen, for a few minutes.

All begin dinner. After a period of no dialogue or specific action MARY JANE *begins the next scene:*

MARY JANE Who's been to the Theatre Royal to see *Carmen*?

KATE The Moody Manners Opera Company.

MARY JANE Moody, yes. Manners, no. But Maria Gay was rather wonderful, I thought. Mr D'Arcy?

MR D'ARCY There was a wonderful contralto in the Irish opera.

JULIA You mean *Muirgeis*.

GABRIEL (*Correcting her pronunciation*) *Muirgheis*.

JULIA The first opera in Irish, by Mr Butler.

MR BROWNE The first opera in Irish? Is it a tragedy?

FREDDY The first opera in Irish! Did you ever hear tell of the likes of it? I don't suppose any of you've laid eyes on the Negro chieftain who's singing in the second part of the pantomime at the Gaiety Theatre? Because now he has one of the very finest tenor voices I myself have ever heard. (*To* BARTELL D'ARCY) Have you heard him?

MR D'ARCY (*Dismissively*) No.

FREDDY Because now I'd be curious to hear your opinion of him. I think he has a grand voice.

MR BROWNE It takes Freddy to find out the really good things.

FREDDY And why couldn't he have a voice too? Is it because he's only a black?

33

MARY JANE Shush, Freddy. No more of that. One of my pupils gave me a pass for *Mignon*. It was very fine but, by golly, did it not make me think of poor Georgina Burns?

MR BROWNE Georgina Burns and her husband, the late Leslie Crotty. A Galway man, if the truth be told. Dead of drink.

FREDDY (*Toasting his mother*) Dead of drink!

MR BROWNE It sends me back farther still, to the old Italian companies that used to come to Dublin: Tietjens, Ilma de Murzka, Campanini, The Great Trebelli, Giuglini, Ravelli, Aramburo. Those were the days when there was something like singing to be heard in Dublin. The top gallery of the old Royal used to be packed night after night. One night an Italian tenor sang five encores to 'Let Me Like a Soldier Fall', introducing a high C every time.

He rises to his feet, and sings:

'Oh let me like a soldier fall
Upon the grassy plain!'
(*Challenging*) Now, Mr D'Arcy, would you complete the aria?

MR D'ARCY I'm as hoarse as a crow. As hoarse as a crow.

MR BROWNE (*Continuing*) The gallery boys would sometimes in their enthusiasm unyoke the horses from the carriage of some great prima donna and pull her themselves through the streets to her hotel. Why do they never play the grand old operas now? *Dinorah*? *Lucrezia Borgia*? I'll tell you why. Because they cannot get their voices to sing them! That's why.

MR D'ARCY I presume there are as good singers today as there were then.

MR BROWNE Where are they?

MR D'ARCY I suppose Caruso, for example, is quite as good, if not better than any of the men you have mentioned.

MARY JANE Oh, I'd give anything to hear Caruso sing. He's so

34

mellifluous.

KATE Would you have some celery, Gabriel? I know you're not a great one for the sweets. I said to Mary Jane, be sure there is celery for Gabriel.

GABRIEL I thank you, Aunt Kate.

FREDDY (*Taking a stalk*) I'm told it's a capital thing for the blood. A capital thing. I'm under a doctor's care at the moment, you know.

MRS MALINS Freddy is going down to Mount Melleray in a week or so. For a bit of a cure.

MR D'ARCY Ah! Mount Melleray. The air down there, very bracing! And the monks are quite hospitable. They never ask for a penny-piece from any of their guests.

MARY JANE They wouldn't want to commit the sin of simony.

MR BROWNE Do you mean to say that a chap can go down there and put up there as if it were a hotel, and live on the fat of the land and then come away without paying anything?

MARY JANE Oh, most people give some donation to the monastery when they leave.

MR BROWNE I wish we had an institution like that in our church. Simony?

MARY JANE 'The buying of ecclesiastical privileges.' We remember it from the Catechism.

KATE You know, the monks never speak. They get up at two in the morning and sleep in their coffins.

MR BROWNE And what do they do that for?

KATE That's the rule of their order.

MR BROWNE Yes, but why?

KATE It's the rule, that's all.

FREDDY The monks . . . you see, the monks are trying to make up for the sins. All the sins committed by all the sinners in the world. The outside world.

MR BROWNE Well, yes. I like that idea very much, but wouldn't a comfortable spring bed do them as well as a coffin?

MARY JANE The coffin is to remind them of their last end.

MRS MALINS They are very good men, the monks. Very pious men.

35

KATE For me, there was only one tenor. To please me, I mean. But I suppose none of you ever heard of him.

MR D'ARCY Who was he, Miss Morkan?

KATE His name was Parkinson. I heard him when he was in his prime and I think he had then the purest tenor voice that was ever put into a man's throat.

MR D'ARCY Strange. I've never even heard of him.

MR BROWNE Yes, yes, Miss Morkan is right. I remember hearing of old Parkinson but he's too far back for me.

KATE A beautiful, pure, sweet, mellow English tenor. Almost as sweet and mellow as our pudding this evening.

FREDDY Speaking of sweet and mellow, Mary Jane, give us a song.

Bashful but ready and all too willing, MARY JANE *rises to sing 'Oh Ye Dead' from Moore's* Melodies. MISS DALY *accompanies her on violin (or piano).*

MARY JANE 'Oh, ye Dead! oh, ye Dead! whom we know by the light you give
From your cold gleaming eyes, though you move like men who live.
Why leave you thus your graves,
In far off fields and waves,
Where the worm and the sea-bird only know your bed,
To haunt this spot where all
Those eyes that wept your fall,
And the hearts that wail'd you, like your own, lie dead?
It is true, it is true, we are shadows cold and wan;
And the fair and the brave whom we lov'd on earth are gone,
But still thus even in death
So sweet the living breath
Of the fields and the flow'rs in our youth we wander'd o'er

That ere, condemn'd, we go
To freeze mid Hecla's snow,
We would taste it awhile, and think we live once
    more!'

GABRIEL Thank you, Mary Jane. Thank you for that. One always wants a little more Moore!

There is a break from the action as the tables are cleared and new plates distributed. AUNT KATE, AUNT JULIA, MARY JANE *and* GRETTA *may help* LILY *to clear. Dessert is served.* MISS DALY *may play additional music.*

JULIA I fear the pudding's not quite brown enough.

MR BROWNE Well, I hope, Miss Morkan, that I'm brown enough for you because, you know, I'm all Browne.

There is a growing and anticipatory silence. A few people pat the table gently as a signal for silence. GABRIEL *pushes back his chair and stands. More patting of the table. Then this ceases altogether.* GABRIEL *taps his glass, leans forward, fingers splayed on the tablecloth. He is smiling nervously.*

GABRIEL Ladies and Gentlemen, it has fallen to my lot this evening, as in years past, to perform a very pleasing task, but a task for which I am afraid my poor powers as a speaker are all too inadequate.

MR BROWNE *(With immense sarcasm)* No! No!

GABRIEL But, however that may be, I can only ask you to-night to take the will for the deed and to lend me your attention for a few moments while I endeavour to express to you in words what my feelings are on this occasion. Ladies and Gentlemen, it is not the first time that we have gathered together under this hospitable roof, around this hospitable board. It is not the first time that we have been the recipients — or perhaps, I had better say, the victims — of the hospitality of certain good ladies.

All laugh and smile at KATE *and* JULIA *and* MARY JANE,
who are pleased and embarrassed by the attention.

I feel more strongly with every recurring year that
our country has no tradition which does it so much
honour and which it should guard so jealously as
that of its hospitality. It is a tradition that is unique
as far as my experience goes (and I have visited
not a few places abroad) among the modern
nations. Some would say, perhaps, that with us it
is rather a failing than anything to be boasted of.
But granted even that, it is, to my mind, a princely
failing, and one that I trust will long be cultivated
among us. Of one thing, at least, I am sure. As long
as this one roof shelters the good ladies aforesaid
— and I wish from my heart it may do so for many
and many a long year to come — the tradition of
genuine warm-hearted courteous Irish hospitality,
which our forefathers have handed down to us
and which we in turn must hand down to our
descendants, is still alive among us.

Applause and a hearty murmur of assent.

Ladies and Gentlemen, a new generation is growing
up in our midst, a generation actuated by new ideas
and new principles. It is serious and enthusiastic
for these new ideas and its enthusiasm, even when
it is misdirected, is, I believe, in the main sincere.
But we are living in a sceptical and, if I may use
the phrase (GABRIEL *pauses*), a thought-tormented
age: and sometimes I fear that this new generation,
educated or hyper-educated as it is, will lack those
qualities of humanity, of hospitality, of kindly
humour which belonged to an older day. Listening
tonight to the names of all those great singers of
the past it seemed to me, I must confess, that we
were living in a less spacious age. Those days might,
without exaggeration, be called spacious days: and

if they are gone beyond recall let us hope, at least, that in gatherings such as this we shall still speak of them with pride and affection, still cherish in our hearts the memory of those dead and gone great ones whose fame the world will not willingly let die.

MR BROWNE Hear! Hear!

GABRIEL But yet, there are always in gatherings such as this sadder thoughts that will recur to our minds: thoughts of the past, of youth, of changes, of absent faces that we miss here tonight. Our path through life is strewn with many such sad memories: and were we to brood upon them always we could not find the heart to go on bravely with our work among the living. We have all of us living duties and living affections which claim, and rightly claim, our strenuous endeavours.

Therefore, I will not linger on the past. I will not let any gloomy moralizing intrude upon us here tonight. Here we are gathered together for a brief moment from the bustle and rush of our everyday routine. We are met here as friends, in the spirit of good fellowship, as colleagues, also to a certain extent, in the true spirit of camaraderie, and as the guests of — what shall I call them? — the Three Graces of the Dublin musical world.

Loud applause. JULIA *turns to* AUNT KATE.

JULIA What did he say?

MARY JANE (*In response*) He says we are the Three Graces, Aunt Julia.

GABRIEL Ladies and Gentlemen, I will not attempt to play tonight the part that Paris played on another occasion. I will not attempt to choose between them. The task would be an invidious one and one beyond my poor powers. For when I view them in turn, whether it be our chief hostess herself, whose good heart, whose too good heart, has become a

39

byword with all who know her, or her sister, who seems to be gifted with perennial youth and whose singing must have been a surprise and a revelation to us all tonight, or, last but not least, when I consider our youngest hostess, talented, cheerful, hard-working and the best of nieces, I confess, Ladies and Gentlemen, that I do not know to which of them I should award the prize. Let us toast them all three together. Let us drink to their health, wealth, long life, happiness and prosperity and may they long continue to hold the proud and self-won position which they hold in their profession and the position of honour and affection which they hold in our hearts.

> *All lift their glasses in toast.* MR BROWNE *begins the song and all join in.* KATE *waves her handkerchief.* FREDDY MALINS *beats time with a fork. Guests should sing along.*

ALL 'For they are jolly gay fellows,
For they are jolly gay fellows,
For they are jolly gay fellows,
Which nobody can deny.
Unless he tells a lie,
Unless he tells a lie,
For they are jolly gay fellows,
For they are jolly gay fellows,
For they are jolly gay fellows,
Which nobody can deny.'
FREDDY *(Getting unsteadily to his feet)* I'm going to run downstairs and start hailing some cabs.

> *He takes in the room, calculating the number of audience members.*

We'll need a slew of them.

> FREDDY *exits the dining room and descends the*

stairs, whistling. His whistling grows fainter and fainter.

MR BROWNE Teddy will have all the cabs in Dublin out.

AUNT KATE Before you leave won't you join us in the next room for a glass of port?

PART THREE

Party Post-dinner. Parlour.

MRS MALINS *is making her preparations to leave.* LILY *brings her cloak.*

MR D'ARCY Miss Daly, I thank you so much for accompanying me.

MISS DALY Well, now, Mr D'Arcy, I haven't accompanied you yet.

MR D'ARCY Am I the only one who thinks Gabriel Conroy might be full of conceit? A little stilted? A little stiff?

MISS DALY A little stiff, Mr D'Arcy. Really!

MR D'ARCY (*Pointing to the wall*) That picture of the balcony scene in *Romeo and Juliet*. The young man gazing up at the young woman's balcony. I'm sure you've had many young men gazing up at your balcony!

MISS DALY All palaver. All palaver, Mr D'Arcy.

> BARTELL D'ARCY *and* MISS DALY *(who now has her violin) move to the staircase and begin to climb towards the third floor. They stop at a point where they are out of the action but visible to the audience.* MRS MALINS *descends the stairs to depart.*

MARY JANE (*To* MR BROWNE) I wouldn't like to face your journey home at this hour.

MR BROWNE I'd like nothing better this minute than a rattling fine walk in the country or a fast drive with a good spanking goer between the shafts.

JULIA (*Sadly*) We used to have a very good horse-and-trap at home.

MARY JANE The never-to-be-forgotten Johnny.

> KATE *and* GABRIEL *laugh.*

42

MR BROWNE Why, what was wonderful about Johnny?

GRETTA Oh no, Gabriel, don't tell it!

GABRIEL The late lamented Patrick Morkan, our grandfather, that is, commonly known in his later years as the old gentleman, was a glue boiler.

KATE (*Laughing*) Oh now, Gabriel, he had a starch mill.

GABRIEL Well, glue or starch, the old gentleman had a horse by the name of Johnny. And Johnny used to work in the old gentleman's mill, walking round and round in order to drive the mill. That was all very well; but now comes the tragic part about Johnny. One fine day the old gentleman thought he'd like to drive out with the quality to a military review in the park.

KATE The Lord have mercy on his soul . . .

GABRIEL Amen. So the old gentleman, as I said, harnessed Johnny and put on his very best tall hat and his very best stock collar and drove out in grand style from his ancestral mansion somewhere near Back Lane, I think.

KATE Oh now, Gabriel, he didn't live in Back Lane, really. Only the mill was there.

GABRIEL Out from the mansion of his forefathers he drove with Johnny. And everything went on beautifully until Johnny came in sight of King Billy's statue, and whether he fell in love with the horse King Billy sits on or whether he thought he was back again in the mill, anyhow he began to walk round the statue.

He walks in a circle around the others.

Round and round he went, and the old gentleman, who was a very pompous old gentleman, was highly indignant. 'Go on, sir! What do you mean, sir! Johnny! Johnny! Most extraordinary conduct! Can't understand the horse!'

MR BROWNE Yes, Johnny understood that in Ireland we're all doomed to go round and round in circles. Everything at a standstill. General paralysis of the insane. To the glorious, pious and immortal soul of . . . Johnny!

FREDDY (*Shouting up from below*) There's nothing moving! I could only get one cab.

MR BROWNE Oh, we'll find another along the quay.

He departs down the stairs. MARY JANE, KATE, JULIA, GRETTA *and* GABRIEL *remain in the main room. Music can now be heard from above.*

GABRIEL Who's playing up there?

KATE Nobody. They're all gone.

MARY JANE Oh no, Aunt Kate. Bartell D'Arcy and Miss Daly aren't gone yet.

From the staircase BARTELL D'ARCY *begins to sing, accompanied by* MISS DALY *on violin.*

MR D'ARCY 'If you'll be the lass of Aughrim
As I'll take you to be
Tell me that first token
That passed between you and me.'

MARY JANE Why it's Bartell D'Arcy! And he wouldn't sing all night.

MR D'ARCY 'Oh don't you remember
That night on yon lean hill
When we both met together
I am sorry now to tell.'

As the song progresses GRETTA *is drawn inexorably to the music-room doorway, where she stands, mesmerized. Gradually she leans against the doorway, utterly focused on the song. (The song itself may be excerpted.)*

'Oh don't you remember
That night on yon lean hill

When we swapped rings off each other's hands
Sorely against my will

Mine was of the beaten gold
Yours was but black tin
The rain falls on my yellow locks
The rain wets my skin

Oh the rain falls on my yellow locks
The rain soaks my skin
My babe lies cold in my arms
Lord Gregory, let me in.

Oh the rain falls on my heavy locks
The rain soaks my skin
My babe lies cold in my arms
But none will let me in.'

The song ends abruptly.

MARY JANE Oh, what a pity.

BARTELL D'ARCY *and* MISS DALY *descend the stairs.*

Oh, Mr D'Arcy, it's downright mean of you to break
off like that when we were all in raptures listening
to you.

JULIA I've been at him all evening, and he told us he had
a dreadful cold and couldn't sing.

KATE Oh, Mr D'Arcy! Now that was a great fib to tell.

MR D'ARCY (*Rudely*) Can't you see that I'm as hoarse as a
crow?

JULIA It's the weather.

KATE Yes, everybody has colds. Everybody!

MARY JANE They say we haven't had snow like it for thirty
years. And I read this morning that snow is general
all over Ireland.

JULIA I love the look of snow.

MARY JANE So do I. I think Christmas is never really Christmas

45

unless we have the snow on the ground.

MISS DALY But poor Mr D'Arcy doesn't like the snow.

LILY brings his coat and BARTELL D'ARCY prepares to depart. GABRIEL increasingly observes GRETTA, who seems lost in thought, much affected. As BARTELL D'ARCY begins to move towards the stairs she suddenly steps forward.

GRETTA Mr D'Arcy, what was the name of that song you were singing?

MR D'ARCY It's called 'The Lass of Aughrim'. But I couldn't remember it properly. Why? Do you know it?

GRETTA 'The Lass of Aughrim.' I couldn't think of the name.

MARY JANE It's a very nice air. (*Sarcastically, to BARTELL D'ARCY*) I'm sorry you were not in voice tonight.

KATE Now, Mary Jane, don't annoy Mr D'Arcy. I won't have him annoyed.

MR D'ARCY Well, goodnight then, Miss Morkan, Miss Morkan. Goodnight, Mr Conroy. Mrs Conroy. Thanks for a pleasant evening. (*Lingeringly*) Goodnight, Miss Daly.

BARTELL D'ARCY departs down the stairs.

MISS DALY Goodnight! Goodnight, Mr D'Arcy.

Crestfallen, she exits.

GRETTA Goodnight.

MARY JANE Come along, Aunt Julia. Let's get you upstairs.

JULIA It was lovely, wasn't it?

GABRIEL Let us help —

GRETTA (*Rousing herself from her reverie*) Yes! Yes, we'll —

MARY JANE Not at all, Gabriel! Aunt Kate and I are entirely capable. Lily is readying your room. It's only a small room.

GRETTA Oh no! Don't trouble over it. We appreciate it so much. It really is too far to go home tonight. Particularly now with the snow.

46

GABRIEL Perhaps we should still go over to the Gresham?
KATE Not at all. You're family, and that's the end of it. Goodnight, Gabriel.
GRETTA Goodnight, Aunt Kate. Goodnight, Aunt Julia.
MARY JANE Goodnight, Gretta. Come along, Aunt Julia.
JULIA Yes, I'm not ashamed to say, I am ready for my bed!

> LILY *appears at the top of the third-floor stairs. Seeing the three women ascend, she goes down to help them. They pass her on the stairs.* LILY *looks down to* GABRIEL *and* GRETTA.

LILY Mr Con-uh-roy, your room is ready. Will you come up?
GABRIEL Thank you, Lily.

> GRETTA *moves first, but slowly, as if not quite awake.* GABRIEL *stands, watching her. He does not begin to cross to the staircase until she is halfway to the third floor. Then he follows.*
> Guests remain on the parlour level. There is a moment of uncertainty as they realize that they are 'alone' for the first time since the play began. LILY, coming down the stairs from above, seems to see them for the first time, or at least for the first time in this new light. Are they still party guests? Or have they become something else? She observes them, and seems to make a decision. Then, solemnly or impishly, she beckons them to follow her upstairs. All ascend the stairs and enter the bedroom.

PART FOUR

In the Bedroom. Third floor.

Guests enter the room to find GABRIEL *standing at the window, look-ing down onto the street.* GRETTA, *seated on the bed, is letting down her hair, removing the pins. Both are lost in their thoughts.*

GABRIEL Gretta! (*She turns to look at him*) You look tired.

GRETTA I am a little.

GABRIEL You don't feel ill or weak?

GRETTA No, tired. That's all.

GABRIEL By the way, Gretta.

GRETTA What is it?

GABRIEL You know that poor fellow Malins?

GRETTA Yes. What about him?

GABRIEL Well, poor fellow, he's a decent sort of chap, after all. He gave me back that sovereign I lent him, and I didn't expect it, really. It's a pity he wouldn't keep away from that Browne, because he's not a bad fellow really.

GRETTA When did you lend him the pound?

GABRIEL Oh, at Christmas, when he opened that little Christmas-card shop in Henry Street.

GRETTA (*After a pause*) You are a very generous person, Gabriel.

> GRETTA *kisses him.* GABRIEL *puts his hands on her hair and begins smoothing it back. For a moment it seems as if they will embrace. He begins to reach out for her.*

GABRIEL Gretta, dear, what are you thinking about?

> GRETTA *does not answer, and she does not let him draw her to him.*

Tell me what it is, Gretta. I think I know what is
the matter. Do I know?

At first GRETTA *does not answer. Then, crying:*

GRETTA Oh! I am thinking about that song. 'The Lass of
Aughrim.'

GRETTA *breaks loose from him and crosses to the bed,
hiding her face.*

GABRIEL What about the song? Why does that make you
cry? Why, Gretta?
GRETTA I am thinking about a person long ago who used
to sing that song.
GABRIEL And who was the person long ago?
GRETTA It was a person I used to know in Galway when I
was living with my grandmother.

GABRIEL, *who has been expecting something else, begins
to lose his smile.*

GABRIEL Someone you were in love with?
GRETTA It was a young boy I used to know. Named
Michael Furey. He used to sing that song. 'The
Lass of Aughrim.' He was very delicate. I can see
him so plainly. Such eyes as he had: big, dark eyes!
And such an expression in them — an expression!
GABRIEL Oh, then you are in love with him?
GRETTA I used to go out walking with him when I was in
Galway.
GABRIEL Perhaps that was why you wanted to go to Galway
with that Ivors girl?
GRETTA (*Surprised*) What for?
GABRIEL How do I know? To see him, perhaps.
GRETTA He is dead. He died when he was only seventeen.
Isn't it a terrible thing to die so young as that?
GABRIEL What was he?
GRETTA He was in the gasworks.

GABRIEL The gasworks?

GRETTA The gasworks.

GABRIEL I suppose you were in love with this Michael Furey, Gretta.

GRETTA I was great with him at that time.

GABRIEL (*Taking* GRETTA's *hand*) And what did he die of so young, Gretta? Consumption, was it?

GRETTA I think he died for me.

GABRIEL *turns away.*

It was in the winter, about the beginning of the winter when I was going to leave my grandmother's and come up here to the convent. And he was ill at the time in his lodgings in Galway and wouldn't be let out, and his people in Oughterard were written to. He was in decline, they said, or something like that. I never knew rightly. Poor fellow. He was very fond of me and he was such a gentle boy. We used to go out together, walking, you know, Gabriel, like the way they do in the country. He was going to study singing only for his health. He had a very good voice, poor Michael Furey.

GABRIEL Well, and then?

GRETTA And then when it came to the time for me to leave Galway and come up to the convent he was much worse and I wouldn't be let see him so I wrote him a letter saying I was going up to Dublin and would be back in the summer, and hoping he would be better then. Then the night before I left I was in my grandmother's house in Nuns' Island, packing up, and I heard gravel thrown up against the window. The window was so wet I couldn't see, so I ran downstairs as I was and slipped out the back into the garden and there was the poor fellow at the end of the garden, shivering.

GABRIEL And did you not tell him to go back?

GRETTA I implored him to go home at once and told him he would get his death in the rain. But he said he did not want to live. I can see his eyes as well as well! He was standing at the end of the wall where there was a tree.

GABRIEL And did he go home?

GRETTA Yes, he went home. And when I was only a week in the convent he died and he was buried in Oughterard, where his people came from. Oh, the day I heard that, that he was dead!

She weeps, overcome by emotion. She flings herself downward on the bed, crying. GABRIEL *holds her hand for another moment, then lets it go. He stands by the bed, watching her. Gradually he understands that she has fallen asleep. He walks to the window and looks out for a long and unsettling moment.*

GABRIEL So you have had that romance in your life, Gretta. A man died for your sake. It hardly pains me now to think how poor a part I, your husband, have played in your life. It's as though we have never lived together as man and wife and, as I think of what you must have been then, in that time of your first girlish beauty, a strange friendly pity for you enters my soul. I do not like to say even to myself that your face is no longer beautiful but I know that it is no longer the face for which Michael Furey braved death. I think of how you who lay beside me had locked in your heart for so many years that image of your lover's eyes when he told you that he did not wish to live. I have never felt like that myself towards any woman but I know that such a feeling must be love. Perhaps you have not told me all the story.

Poor Aunt Julia! She will soon be a shade with the shade of Patrick Morkan and his horse. I caught that haggard look upon her face for a moment when she was singing 'Arrayed for the Bridal'. Soon, perhaps, I will be sitting in that same drawing room, dressed in black, my silk hat on my knees. The blinds will be drawn down and Aunt Kate will be sitting beside me, crying and blowing her nose and telling me how Julia has died. I will cast about in my mind for some words that might console her, and I'll find only lame and useless ones. Yes, yes: that will happen very soon.

One by one we are all becoming shades. Better pass boldly into that other world, in the full glory of some passion, than fade and wither dismally with age.

I imagine I see the form of a young man standing under a dripping tree. And other forms are near. My soul has approached that region where dwell the vast hosts of the dead. I am conscious of, but cannot apprehend, their wayward and flickering existence. My own identity is fading out into a grey impalpable world: the solid world itself which these dead had one time reared and lived in is dissolving and dwindling.

GABRIEL *makes his way to the window.*

It has begun to snow again. The flakes, silver and dark, falling obliquely against the lamplight. The time has come for me to set out on my journey westward. Yes, the newspapers are right: snow is general all over Ireland. It is falling on every part of the dark central plain, on the treeless hills, falling softly upon the Bog of Allen and, farther westward, softly falling into the dark mutinous Shannon waves. It is falling, too, upon every part of the lonely churchyard on the hill where Michael Furey lies buried. It lies thickly drifted on the crooked crosses and headstones, on the spears of the little gate, on the barren thorns. My soul swoons slowly as I hear the snow falling faintly through the universe and faintly falling, like the descent of their last end, upon all the living and the dead.

MICHAEL FUREY/BARTELL D'ARCY (*Heard from else-where, not in the room itself*):

'Oh the rain falls on my yellow locks
The rain soaks my skin
My babe lies cold in my arms
Lord Gregory, let me in.

Oh the rain falls on my heavy locks
The rain soaks my skin
My babe lies cold in my arms
But none will let me in.'

> GABRIEL *stretches out and lies down beside* GRETTA, *pulling a sheet over them both.*

> *Guests descend to parlour level, then to Entryway/Lobby, and depart.*
> *Curtain call may take place in the bedroom or on the parlour level.*

Alternate Staging for Opening Scene

For venues in which audience members will enter on the parlour floor or into the parlour itself, the following staging may work best.

Entryway/Lobby of Miss Kate and Miss Julia Morkan's Georgian home in Dublin.
Music can be heard from a nearby piano, also the stamping and shuffling of feet. A party is underway.

Guests (audience members) enter, are fussed over by LILY, *the maid, who helps them off with their coats which she hands to another servant who checks them and returns the coat check to the guest.*

> LILY (*Speaking variously to newly arrived guests*) That's the way now. I'll be having your coat, m'am. What a terrible night! Ah, the Misses Morkan were just asking after you. We'll just wait down here for a bit, they're finishing up upstairs. Did you hear that Bartell D'Arcy himself is here tonight! Where is that Gabriel Con-uh-roy? The Misses were asking after him. I hope that Freddy Malins doesn't turn up screwed. You know he's sometimes hard to manage when he's screwed.

> *From time to time we can hear* KATE MORKAN *and* JULIA MORKAN *calling from the parlour:* Who is here? Who's that, Lily? Who's come? Is it Gabriel?
> *When the complete audience of guests have arrived and handed over their coats to the coat check* LILY *addresses them with words from the opening line of 'The Dead':*

> LILY I am run off my feet. Literally run off my feet!
> KATE Is he here yet, Lily? Is Gabriel here?
> LILY (*Exasperated*) No, Miss Kate, not yet.

There is a loud knock at the door. LILY *rushes to it and opens the door to* GABRIEL *and* GRETTA.

LILY Oh, Mr Con-uh-roy. Miss Kate and Miss Julia thought you were never coming. (*As they enter*) Goodnight, Mrs Con-uh-roy.

GABRIEL *stamps his feet to dislodge snow from his galoshes.*

GABRIEL I'll engage they did. But they forget that my wife here takes three mortal hours to dress herself.

LILY (*Leading* GRETTA *to the foot of the stairs*) Miss Kate! Miss Julia! Here's Mrs Con-uh-roy!

JULIA *and* KATE *come briskly down the stairs. Both kiss* GRETTA.

KATE You must be perished alive!

JULIA Is Gabriel with you?

GABRIEL Here I am, as right as the mail, Aunt Julia! Go on up, I'll follow.

GRETTA, JULIA *and* KATE *ascend the stairs to the party. Focus now returns to* GABRIEL *and* LILY, *still in the foyer.* GABRIEL *sits.* LILY *is attempting to help him with his galoshes.*

LILY Is it snowing again, Mr Con-uh-roy?

GABRIEL Yes, Lily, and I think we're in for a night of it.

He looks up at the ceiling, listening to the music and movement from above, then back at LILY.

Con-uh-roy. You make me sound like some ancient Irish king.

LILY Miss Kate always says your mother was the brains-carrier of the family.

GABRIEL Conroy. Two syllables are quite enough. Tell me,

Lily, do you still go to school?

LILY   Oh no, sir. I'm done schooling this year and more.

GABRIEL   Oh then, I suppose we'll be going to your wedding one of these fine days with your young man, eh?

LILY   (*Bitterly*) The men that is now is only all palaver and what they can get out of you.

> GABRIEL *is embarrassed, aware that he has said something wrong, but unclear as to what. He kicks at his galoshes to get them off, adjusts his clothing. He fumbles for a coin in his pocket.*

GABRIEL   Oh Lily, it's Christmastime, isn't it? Just . . . here's a little . . .

LILY   Oh no, sir! I wouldn't take it.

> GABRIEL, *escaping quickly towards the stairs, waves at* LILY.

GABRIEL   Christmastime! Christmastime!

LILY   Well, thank you, sir.

> GABRIEL *ascends the stairs. After he disappears* LILY *begins to gather the guests and direct them up the staircase.*

(*To guests*) Well, let's get along upstairs. Come along, the Misses Morkan will be wanting to start!

Food and Dining

In James Joyce's 'The Dead', dinner is thus described: 'A fat brown goose lay at one end of the table and at the other end, on a bed of creased paper strewn with sprigs of parsley, lay a great ham, stripped of its outer skin and peppered over with crust crumbs, a neat paper frill round its shin and beside this was a round of spiced beef. Between these rival ends ran parallel lines of side-dishes: two little minsters of jelly, red and yellow; a shallow dish full of blocks of blancmange and red jam, a large green leaf-shaped dish with a stalk-shaped handle, on which lay bunches of purple raisins and peeled almonds, a companion dish on which lay a solid rectangle of Smyrna figs, a dish of custard topped with grated nutmeg, a small bowl full of chocolates and sweets wrapped in gold and silver papers and a glass vase in which stood some tall celery stalks. In the centre of the table there stood, as sentries to a fruit-stand which upheld a pyramid of oranges and American apples, two squat old-fashioned decanters of cut glass, one containing port and the other dark sherry. On the closed square piano a pudding in a huge yellow dish lay in waiting and behind it were three squads of bottles of stout and ale and minerals, drawn up according to the colours of their uniforms, the first two black, with brown and red labels, the third and smallest squad white, with transverse green sashes.'

Dessert is described as follows: 'The huge pudding was transferred to the table . . . Gabriel's wife served out spoonfuls of the pudding and passed the plates down the table. Midway down they were held up by Mary Jane, who replenished them with raspberry or orange jelly or with blancmange and jam.'

Effort should be made to maintain the flavours and atmosphere of an Edwardian meal, including, if possible, the use of vintage glassware, cutlery and dishes.

The actors' table should be placed in the middle of the room, with long tables around the periphery of the room at which audience members can be seated facing in, to enjoy an un-impeded view of the dinner scene. Waitstaff should coordinate service to take advantage of the non-scripted portions of the meal, and refrain from entering the room during the scripted portions of the scene. Arrangement of tables may be adjusted according to the shape and size of a venue's dining room, so long as the focus is on visibility and ease of service. Four members of the audience may be seated at the actors' table during the dinner scene. As audience members enter the dining room, seating is best facilitated by a cast member, rather than by waitstaff.

Music

As guests enter the Misses Morkan's party, Miss Daly or Mary Jane may be at the piano, playing the Victorian parlour music that would have been popular at the time. A likely source of this music would be Thomas Moore's *Irish Melodies*, traditional Irish tunes to which Thomas Moore (1779-1852) contributed new lyrics, and which were published in ten volumes between 1808-1834. Some of the most popular of these include 'The Minstrel Boy' and 'The Last Rose of Summer'. Later arrangements of these songs were published in the 1850s. Thomas Moore's *Irish Melodies* are widely available, though any period music that might have been sung in 1904 can be substituted.

Miss Daly's 'Academy Piece': Attributed in the original story to Mary Jane and played on the piano, *The Dead, 1904* instead assigns this song to Miss Daly. The initial production had Mary Jane play a violin piece because of that particular cast member's musical strengths, but the 'Academy Piece' may be either violin or piano music. In the original text the song is long and 'full of runs and difficult passages'. Gabriel finds the performance irritating and somewhat boring and notes that the only person who seems to follow it is the musician herself though he claps enthusiastically. The piece ends with 'runs of scales' and 'a trill of octaves in the treble and a final deep octave in the bass'. The initial production selected the cadenza from the Sibelius *Violin Concerto in D minor, Opus 47* (1904). Any appropriately showy or complex music for piano or violin that pre-dates 1904 may be selected.

Miss Julia Morkan's song, 'Arrayed for the Bridal': Words by George Linley (1798-1865) to the music of the aria 'Son vergin vezzosa' from the opera *I Puritani* by Vincenzo Bellini (1801-1835).

Mary Jane's song, 'O Ye Dead': From Thomas Moore's *Irish Melodies*. It is likely that the novella's title comes from this song.

Incidental dinner music (Miss Daly): In the initial production Miss Daly plays Irish traditional fiddle music as dinner plates are cleared and dessert is served.

Bartell D'Arcy's song, 'The Lass of Aughrim': Miss Daly may accompany Mr D'Arcy on violin or on piano, as staging and musicianship allow. The music most closely associated with Joyce's 'The Dead', 'The Lass of Aughrim' is an Irish version of the Scottish ballad, 'The Lass of Roch Royal'. *The Dead, 1904* emphasizes the song's allusion to Lord William Henry Gregory, and to his activities during the Irish Famine. (Lord Gregory was the author of the 'Gregory Clause' of the 1847 relief laws, which exempted from relief anybody who owned more than a quarter of an acre of land. Many unscrupulous landlords used the Gregory Clause as an excuse to evict destitute tenants who were then forced to go into the workhouses or to emigrate.) There are many variations of the song.